MONSTER BOOK OF GOD'S LOVE

Fun, low-prep puppet skits to help children learn & LIVE GOD'S WORD!

Puppets for JESUS!
Winning the lost, strengthening faith
& equipping the saints through
the power of God's word.
PuppetsForJESUS.com

Scriptures taken from the Holy Bible,
New International Version®, NIV®.
Copyright © 1973, 1978, 1984 by Biblica, Inc.™
Used by permission of Zondervan.
All rights reserved worldwide.
www.zondervan.com

Copyright © Puppets for JESUS! PuppetsForJESUS.com All rights reserved

The skits in this book may be copied and reproduced for the use of performing the skits contained within for non-profit Christian ministry only. No further permission is required to use the skits contained within for non-profit Christian ministry. The materials in this book may only be used as listed above and may not be used in any efforts to contradict any portion of the contents of this publication. No portion of this publication may be published, transmitted, reproduced, or distributed in any form including but not limited to internet, electrical, mechanical, photocopying, recording, or any other form without prior written consent from the publisher.

CONTENTS

Meet the Monsters 4

Break the Chains and Believe - Acts 16:31 5

Forget about it; Jesus is the Way - John 14:6 8

Cross Over Today - John 5:24 11

For God So Loved the World - John 3:16 13

Monster Strength - Exodus 15:2 16

Eternal Life… Got it? Get it? Good! - Romans 6:23 18

An Old Bed and a New Heart - 2 Corinthians 5:17 21

Hairy People Must Confess - Romans 10:10 23

Sin & Toenails - Romans 3:23 25

Rollin' with the Rock - 2 Samuel 22:47 28

Sing it! Shout it! Tell it! - 1 Chronicles 16:9 29

Tell ALL - Psalms 9:1 30

MEET THE MONSTERS

Each puppet skit consists of two main monster characters, Moe and Harry. Moe is one slick city Monster from New York. He has a strong New York accent, and he might be a little rough around the edges at times, but he is always ready to help the kids memorize the Bible verse with his faithful furry friend, Harry. Harry isn't a big city monster like Moe, and although his accent might seem a little dopey and it may take him a little longer to catch on to what's going on, he is quick at learning God's word and helping others do the same.

Tips for the puppeteer performing Moe:

- ✓ Practice your New York accent by saying some of Moe's common catch phrases such as, "Forget about it!" and "Bada-bing bada-boom!".

- ✓ Remember, Moe is the brains of the operation and although he's one tough ball of fur and a bit of a wise guy, he's never mean.

- ✓ Moe's movements are a little quicker and sharper than Harry's since he's a big city monster.

- ✓ He's an incredibly strong monster because he works out by lifting huge monster weights. Sometimes, he'll give Harry a little pat on the back to encourage him, but it usually sends his furry pal flying because he just doesn't know his own strength.

- ✓ He uses his hands a lot when he talks, so pump up them puppeteering muscles and practice using the arm-rods!

Tips for the puppeteer performing Harry:

- ✓ Practice your dopey and cartoon-like character voice by voicing up some of Harry's common sounds and phrases. When Harry is thinking or confused, he often hesitates out loud by making the sound of, "Uhhh" and he sometimes uses phrases such as, "Golly gee".

- ✓ Harry's movements are not as face paced as Moe's unless he gets excited, which he quite often does.

- ✓ Sometimes, he gets confused and needs to scratch his head while he is thinking.

- ✓ Harry really loves food and every time he talks about it, he can't help but to rub his belly, so make sure he is well fed before each show!

BREAK THE CHAINS AND BELIEVE
ACTS 16:31

Moe: Today we're going to be talking about some monster chains.

Harry: Like some big gold chains that you wear around your neck? Some bling-blang?

Moe: It's bling-bling and that is not the chains that we are talking about.

Harry: Uhh, what were we talking about? I forget.

Moe: How surprising...

Harry: What's the surprise?

Moe: I'll tell ya. The Bible tells us that there was a big surprise for two men named Paul and Silas.

Harry: Those guys were put in prison for telling people about Jesus. Hey, those guys were put in chains too. We should tell the kids about those chains.

Moe: Gee, Harry, ya think?

Harry: Well yeah, Moe. Even though they were chained up and thrown into prison, they would not stop praising God. They were praying and singing all night.

Moe: The other prisoners were listening to them, and then something monsterly happened. While they were singing: the earth started to shake, the prison door swung open, and everyone's chains came loose!

Harry: Ooooooo the prison guard is in trouble! Make that a double!

Moe: Yeah, when he saw that door open, he was so scared about what the king would do to him that he took out his sword and was about to kill himself with it!

Harry: Oh noooo, I hate that part. Don't tell me. That is scarier than monsters hiding under my bed.

Moe: What do you mean? You are a monster.

Harry: But I still don't want any hiding under my bed.

Moe: Well don't worry, Nobody escaped and the guard didn't off himself. Paul yelled out to the guard, Paul said, Dude, don't hurt yourself, we are all here, man!

Harry: Uh, I don't remember it quite like that.

Moe: Well, I monstered it up a little. The guard fell down trembling before Paul and Silas and asked them what he must do to be saved.

Harry: What did they tell them?

Moe: *They replied, "Believe in the Lord Jesus, and you will be saved, you and your household."*

Harry: Hey, that sounds like our Bible verse, *Acts 16:31*.

Moe: That's because it is *Acts 16:31*.

Harry: Wow! Whatever happened to the guard?

Moe: He brought Paul and Silas over to his house to eat, and he was so filled with joy because he and his family were saved.

Harry: Uhh, I wonder what they ate.

Moe: Food, Taco Bell, maybe.

Harry: Food is my favorite.

Moe: Let's learn this verse. Repeat after me.

Harry: Kids, repeat the verse with me!

Moe: *Acts 16:31…*

Harry: (repeat with kids)

Moe: *They replied, "Believe in the Lord Jesus, and you will be saved..."*

Harry: (repeat with kids)

Moe: "...you and your household."

Harry: (repeat with kids) I still wonder about it though.

Moe: What's that?

Harry: I wonder what they ate. Do you think it could have been pizza?

Moe: You know what?

Harry: What?

Moe: I'm going to hide under your bed tonight. (exit)

Harry: Noooooooooooooo! (exit)

FORGET ABOUT IT: JESUS IS THE WAY!
JOHN 14:6

Moe: Are you ready?

Harry: I'm ready! Uhh... ready for what?

Moe: To learn this monster Bible verse!

Harry: There were monsters in the Bible?

Moe: Noooo.

Harry: Well, you just said…

Moe: Forget about it.

Harry: Okay, but you said it.

Moe: Now I'm saying John 14:6

Harry: John 14:6?

Moe: Yeah, the Bible verse, John 14:6.

Harry: Was John 14:6 about a monster?

Moe: No. Forget about the monsters already.

Harry: I'll try, but it will be hard.

Moe: Just repeat after me and forget about it.

Harry: Forget about the Bible verse? I thought we were supposed to memorize it.

Moe: Yes, memorize it.

Harry: But you said to forget about it.

Moe: I meant about the monsters.

Harry: I forgot about it, but then you brought it up again!

Moe: Just repeat this verse after me so we can memorize it.

Harry: Got it.

Moe: *John 14:6...*

Harry: *John 14:16...*

Moe: *Jesus answered,*

Harry: Who was Jesus talking to?

Moe: You are supposed to repeat after me.

Harry: But I can't help but wonder who Jesus was talking to.

Moe: Jesus was talking to His disciples. Jesus knew that He would soon be dying for the sins of the world, and that he would be going to heaven to be with God the Father. The disciples wanted to know the way to heaven so they could be with Jesus.

Harry: Jesus is the only way to heaven; Jesus says so in John 14:6.

Moe: So, let's learn us some John 14:16! Kids, show Harry how it is done. Repeat the verse after me. *John 14:6...*

Harry: (repeat after kids)

Moe: *Jesus answered, "I am the way and the truth and the life...*

Harry: (repeat after kids)

Moe: *No one comes to the Father except through me.*

Harry: (repeat after kids)

Moe: *John 14:6.*

Harry: (repeat after kids) Thanks boy and girls!

Harry and Moe: Bye! (exit)

CROSS OVER TODAY!
JOHN 5:24

Moe: Today is the day!

Harry: Today is always today.

Moe: No, man. Today isn't today.

Harry: Uh, what do you mean? How can today not be today?

Moe: Today is today.

Harry: You said it wasn't.

Moe: What I am trying to say is, today is THE day.

Harry: Oh, well why didn't you say that to begin with.

Moe: I did.

Harry: I'm confused!

Moe: We know.

Harry: So?

Moe: So what?

Harry: What is today, besides today?

Moe: Today is the day that we learn our Bible verse and today could be the day that some of these kids cross over from death to life.

Harry: When you accept Jesus into your heart, you cross over from death to life.

Moe: That is right! If you don't have Jesus then you are heading down a road that leads to death, but the moment you accept Jesus as your personal Lord and Savior, then you cross over onto the road that leads to life.

Harry: In *John 5:24*, Jesus says, *I tell you the truth, whoever hears my word and believes him who sent me has eternal life and will not be condemned; he has crossed over from death to life.*

Moe: I'm so monsterly proud of you, but I think the girls can say it louder than that.

Harry: Let's find out. Come on girls, up on your feet!

Moe: Repeat after me. *John 5:24... I tell you the truth... whoever hears my word and believes him who sent me... has eternal life and will not be condemned... he has crossed over from death to life.*

Harry: Wow! Great job. Take a bow and take a seat. I don't think the boys could do better than that!

Moe: I don't know about that. Why don't we find out?

Harry: Good idea. Okay boys, up on your feet. Repeat after me and blow our fur off! *John 5:24... I tell you the truth... whoever hears my word and believes him who sent me... has eternal life and will not be condemned... he has crossed over from death to life.*

Moe: Monsterly loud! Give yourselves a pat on the back and have a seat. Great job! I think I better go and rearrange my fur; you blew us away! See you next time! (exit)

Harry: Bye boys and girls! See ya soooooon! (exit)

FOR GOD SO LOVED THE WORLD
JOHN 3:16

Moe: Okay! Let's do this!

Harry: Uhh, do what?

Moe: What we came here for.

Harry: And that would be?

Moe: To help with the Bible verse. What kind of monster are you anyways?

Harry: A hairy one. That's why they named me Harry. Gee Moe, I thought you knew that.

Moe: Yeah... okay. Let's get this show on the road!

Harry: On the road? I thought we were doing the show right here. Where are we going, Moe?

Moe: I meant let's get started.

Harry: Why didn't you just say let's get started then?

Moe: I did!

Harry: Oh no you didn't.

Moe: Well I am saying it now. Let's get started!

Harry: Okay!

Moe: Listen up boys and girls, Monster Moe here.

Harry: And hairy Harry here!

Moe: Hairy Harry here?

Harry: Yeah. I'm hairy, my name is Harry, and I'm here.

Moe: Okay, whatever. Just repeat after me and the boys and girls can repeat after you. Got it?

Harry: Uh, I think so.

Moe: Good!

Harry: Good! Now repeat after me boys and girls.

Moe: Not yet!

Harry: Not yet. Your turn boys and girls. Whatever I say repeat after me.

Moe: Whatever! Let's just get started.

Harry: Whatever! Let's just get started.

Moe: Ughhhh!

Harry: Ughhh!

Moe: *John 3:16...*

Harry: *John 3:16 ...*

Moe: *For God so loved the world...*

Harry: *For God so loved the world...*

Moe: *that He gave His one and only Son...*

Harry: *that He gave His one and only Son...*

Moe: *that whoever believes in Him...*

Harry: *that whoever believes in Him...*

Moe: *shall not perish but have eternal life...*

Harry: *shall not perish but have eternal life...*

Moe: *John 3:16*

Harry: *John 3:16! John 3:16! John 3:16!*

Moe: Why are you saying *John 3:16* over and over again?

Harry: So I can remember it, duh.

Moe: That's the smartest thing you've said today!

Harry: Well, thank you. I think.

Moe: See ya later kids! Monster Moe is outta here. (exit)

Harry: See ya soon! (exit)

MONSTER STRENGTH
EXODUS 15:2

Moe: Can you believe it? I am stronger than ever!

Harry: Sure, rub it in.

Moe: Aww, come on, Harry. I'm just excited that I am able to bench-press five hundred monster pounds!

Harry: Well, I am not even able to bench-press five unmonsterous pounds! I feel bad.

Moe: You don't need to feel bad. You have a lot of strength on the inside.

Harry: On the inside?

Moe: Yeah man. Jesus is your strength.

Harry: Will Jesus give me the strength to bench-press 500 monster pounds?

Moe: Perhaps, if you need to, but that is not the kind of strength that I am talking about.

Harry: Well what kind of strength are you talking about?

Moe: When you accept Jesus, God the Son, God's Holy Spirit comes to live inside of you.

Harry: God's Holy Spirit makes you strong and brave.

Moe: That's right! God's Holy Spirit will fill your life with joy and peace.

Harry: I understand. The Holy Spirit will give me strength! The Holy Spirit gives us strength to face every challenge and every problem that life brings our way.

Moe: The *Lord is my strength and my song; He has become my salvation.*

Harry: *Exodus 15:2.* That is our Bible verse. *Exodus 15:2, The Lord is my strength and my song; He has become my salvation.*

Moe: Come on kids! Repeat after us as loudly as you can. *Exodus 15:2. The Lord is my strength and my song;*

Harry: *He has become my salvation!*

Moe: Great job! Give yourselves a monster pat on the back!

Harry: See ya next time boys and girls! Byeeeeeeeeeee! (exit)

Moe: Keep learning those Bible verses and stay strong! (exit)

ETERNAL LIFE... GOT IT? GET IT? GOOD!
ROMANS 6:23

Moe: Monster Moe coming at ya!

Harry: And I'm Harry the hairy monster!

Moe: Let's rock out this monster verse!

Harry: I've been studying it. I know this one.

Moe: *Romans 6:23!*

Harry: *Romans 6:23*, yep yep yep, that's the verse alright. *Romans 6:23* is fine by me.

Moe: Hey, I'm proud of you; that rhymes. *Romans 6:23* is fine by me.

Harry: Yeah, rhyming helps me remember. *Romans 6:23* is fine by me!

Moe: Well *Romans 6:23* is just fine by me too. Show us what ya got!

Harry: What do I have?

Moe: The verse.

Harry: Oh. Where is it?

Moe: Hopefully it is in your memory.

Harry: Oh yeah. What verse was it.

Moe: *Romans 6:23.*

Harry: *Romans 6:23* is fine by me.

Moe: Well, why don't you share it with the rest of us?

Harry: Share what?

Moe: The verse!

Harry: Sure. *Romans 6:23, For the wages of sin is death, but the gift of God is eternal life in Christ Jesus our Lord. Romans 6:23.*

Moe: Amazing!

Harry: Thank you.

Moe: Don't mention it!

Harry: I already did.

Moe: Okay kids, hear me hear me! Harry is going to say the verse and we'll repeat after him. Got it? Get it? Good! Repeat after Harry when he says the Bible verse. Alright Harry, give us what ya got!

Harry: What do I have? Did you see a flea? Why would you want fleas? I had them once. I will never forget it. They itch! Monster fleas are the worst kind!

Moe: I'm not talking about fleas!

Harry: Monster fleas?

Moe: No!

Harry: What are you talking about then?

Moe: The Bible verse.

Harry: I should have the kids repeat it after me.

Moe: Ya think?

Harry: Sure. Everybody repeat after me. *Romans 6:23!*

Moe: (repeat with kids)

Harry: *For the wages of sin is death...*

Moe: (repeat with kids)

Harry: *But the gift of God is eternal life through Christ Jesus our Lord.*

Moe: (repeat witn kids) Now ya got it!

Harry: Got what? Fleas? Did you see one?

Moe: I'm outta here! (exit)

Harry: I think I'm starting to itch! (exit)

AN OLD BED AND A NEW HEART
2 CORINTHIANS 5:17

Harry: Finally!

Moe: Finally what?

Harry: I finally threw my bed away!

Moe: Where are you going to sleep?

Harry: In my bed?

Moe: I don't understand. I thought you threw it away.

Harry: I did. It was horrible. It was dirty and had holes in it. Springs were popping out everywhere!

Moe: If you threw it out, how are you going to sleep in it?

Harry: I'm not.

Moe: I'm sooo confused. You're not going to sleep in it? You just said you were going to sleep in it.

Harry: I am not going to sleep in my old bed, I am going to sleep in my brand new comfy bed. The old one has gone and the new has come!

Moe: Why didn't you just say that in the first place?

Harry: I don't know. I thought I did.

Moe: Okay, whatever. Hey, that reminds me of our Bible verse.

Harry: My beds remind you of our Bible verse?

Moe: Yeah. You had an old dirty bed and traded it in for a brand new one. In *2 Corinthians 5:17*, the Bible tells us if we accept Jesus then our old sinful self goes away and we are made brand new!

Harry: Yep, that's true because every bit of God's word is the truth! *2 Corinthians 5:17, Therefore, if anyone is in Christ, he is a new creation; the old has gone, the new has come!*

Moe: That is right! That is exactly what it says in *2 Corinthians 5:17, Therefore, if anyone is in Christ, he is a new creation; the old has gone, the new has come!*

Harry: That is even more exciting than my new bed!

Moe: Bye everybody! (exit)

Harry: See ya sooooon! (exit)

HAIRY PEOPLE MUST CONFESS
ROMANS 10:10

Moe: Hear me! Hear me!

Harry: I hear you. I hear you.

Moe: I want the kids to hear me.

Harry: I am pretty sure they do, but I am not sure if they want to be called kids.

Moe: What would I call them?

Harry: Age challenged.

Moe: That's just ridiculous.

Harry: I'm just saying.

Moe: Well don't say.

Harry: Don't say what?

Moe: Don't say we ever had this discussion.

Harry: Uhh, what discussion?

Moe: Exactly!

Harry: Uhh, I don't get it.

Moe: We know.

Harry: Um, what do you know?

Moe: I know this Bible verse.

Harry: Well, let's learn it then.

Moe: Okay kids, if you have blonde hair, stand up and repeat after me. *Romans 10:10... For it is with your heart that you believe and are justified.... and it is with your mouth that you confess and are saved... Romans 10:10.*

Harry: My turn, my turn. Hairy me! Hairy me!

Moe: I think you mean hear me hear me.

Harry: No, I mean hairy me hairy me.

Moe: What does that have to do with our Bible verse?

Harry: I am confessing it with my mouth.

Moe: Confessing you are hairy?

Harry: Yeah.

Moe: You are supposed to confess that you have given your life to Jesus, not that you are hairy.

Harry: Ooops. I just love hairy people. The hairier the better I always say. So, all the kids that have hair on their arms stand up and repeat after me. Wow! This is one hairy crowd. *Romans 10:10... For it is with your heart that you believe and are justified... and it is with your mouth that you confess and are saved... Romans 10:10*

Moe: I hate to admit it, but I agree with you, hairy people are the best. Everybody that has hair in their nose or above their eyes stand up! You guys a bunch of fur balls! You must be part monster! Repeat after me, *Romans 10:10... For it is with your heart that you believe and are justified... and it is with your mouth that you confess and are saved. Romans 10:10*

Hairy: Uhhh, I think I need to go get my fur trimmed.

Moe: I'm going to get mine styled.

Hairy: Stay hairy boys and girls! (exit)

Moe: Keep growing that fur! (exit)

SIN AND TOENAILS
ROMANS 3:23

Moe: Okay, I got questions and I want answers.

Harry: What do ya wanna know, Moe? That rhymes. What do you know, Moe, I'm a poet and now you know it!

Moe: Yeah, hysterical. I got to ask these shorties some questions.

Harry: Shorties?

Moe: Yeah, you know, curtain climbers, tricycle motors, kids, kiddos, little bambinos. They're small, they're short, they're shorties. Get? Got it? Good!

Harry: Uhhh, I don't think that's very nice.

Moe: What's not nice?

Harry: Calling them shorties, that's not nice.

Moe: What should I call them then?

Harry: Vertically challenged would be more appropriate.

Moe: I'm about to challenge you in a second if you don't put a sock in it.

Harry: In what?

Moe: Just forget about it. Okay shorties, listen up… If you like raspberries stand up. Sit down.

Harry: Ask them if they like spinach.

Moe: If you like spinach stand up. Okay, sit down.

Harry: I know... If you ever ate toenails stand up!

Moe: That's sick!

Harry: Well, how else would I trim them?

Moe: Just change the subject. If you ever rode a roller coaster, stand up. Awesome! Okay, sit down.

Harry: If you ever rode a horse, stand up. Spin around and sit down. Uhh Moe, I have a question for you.

Moe: What's that?

Harry: Why are we asking these questions?

Moe: Because I got a plan. Monster Moe always has a plan.

Harry: What's the plan?

Moe: Ya see, some kids like raspberries, but some don't. Some of these shorties rode on a roller coaster but not all of them, but there is one thing that all of us have done.

Harry: Trimmed our toenails with our teeth?

Moe: No, man. Gross! *Romans 3:23, For ALL have sinned and fall short of the glory of God.*

Harry: *Romans 3:23* says, for *ALL have sinned and fall short of the glory of God.*

Moe: Yep. *Romans 3:23* says, *For ALL have sinned and fall short of the glory of God.* All of us have sinned, every single one of us.

Harry: All of us can be forgiven of our sins, too. All ya gotta do is repent and ask Jesus to forgive you.

Moe: That's right! Repenting means we are sorry for our sins, so we turn away from them and do our best to stop sinning. *Romans 3:23* says, *For ALL have sinned and fall short of the glory of God,* but all we have to do is ask Jesus to come into our hearts and forgive us of our sins and bada-bing bada-boom our sins are all gone!

Harry: God washes us clean from all our sins and totally forgets our sins too!

Moe: You got it. And because *Romans 3:23* tells us, *For ALL have sinned and fall short of the glory of God*, we ALL need Jesus.

Harry: I have a question. Do you think eating toenails is a sin? I really hope not.

Moe: It's definitely disgusting! Gross! I'm outta here! (exit)

Harry: Wait, everybody has different tastes. Don't knock it until you have tried it! (exit)

ROLLIN' WITH THE ROCK!
2 SAMUEL 22:47

Moe: Rocking oh yeah! I'm rocking it! There is no other way to go… Rock it! Rock it! ROCK IT!

Harry: Rocket? Are you flying to the moon on a rocket ship?

Moe: Naw man. I'm rocking it. Rollin' with the rock! Everybody should rock it!

Harry: Rock what? The boat? You know I don't like boats. I hate getting wet!

Moe: I'm talking about rollin' with the rock, baby fur.

Harry: Rocket ships? Boats? Rolling around with rocks? I'm confusededed!

Moe: What's new?

Harry: Salvation makes ya brand new.

Moe: Now you're diggin it!

Harry: Digging up rocks?

Moe: Digging THE ROCK! I am praising the Rock of My Salvation!

Harry: I get! I get! JESUS is the Rock! You're rollin' with the Rock and you're walking with God! *2 Samuel 22:47, The LORD lives! Praise be to my Rock! Exalted be God, the Rock, my Savior!*

Moe: I'll roll with that! *2 Samuel 22:47, The LORD lives! Praise be to my Rock! Exalted be God, the Rock, my Savior!*

Harry: Come on everybody, roll with us! Exalt the Rock! Repeat after me! *2 Samuel 22:47… The Lord lives… Praise be to my Rock… Exalted be God… the Rock, my Savior!*

Moe: I gotta roll! (exit)

Harry: A sweet roll? A dinner roll? A sticky roll? I'm hungry! What kind of roll do ya got? Wait up! (exit)

SING IT! SHOUT IT! TELL IT!
1 CHRONICLES 16:9

Moe: Come on everybody! Up on your feet!

Harry: (singing) *Sing to Him, sing praise to Him; tell of all His wonderful acts!*

Moe: Sing it! *1 Chronicles 16:9!*

Harry: Sing after us! *1 Chronicles 16:9!*

Moe: Louder! *1 Chronicles 16:9!* Sing *to Him... sing praise to Him... tell of all His wonderful acts!*

Harry: (singing loudly) Louder! Louder! Louder! *1 Chronicles 16:9!*

Moe: *Sing to Him... sing praise to Him... tell of all His wonderful acts!*

Harry: Sing! Sing! Sing! Sing *Sing to Him... sing praise to Him... tell of all His wonderful acts!*

Moe: *1 Chronicles 16:9*

Harry: (bowing) Take a seat, but first take a bow!

Moe: And remember to always bow your heads in prayer, and take time to *Sing to Him...*

Harry: *Sing praise to Him!*

Moe: *Tell of all His wonderful acts!*

Harry: *1 Chronicles 16:9*

Moe: (Singing) I've been singing praises to my God, but now I have to go tell of all His wonderful acts! Later, peach fuzzies! (exit)

Harry: Bye, boys and girls! God has done a lot so there is a lot to sing about and tell about! See ya next time! (exit)

TELL ALL!
PSALMS 9:1

Harry: Guess what?

Moe: What?

Harry: I said, guess.

Moe: You're running for president?

Harry: Close!

Moe: Mayor of Furryville?

Harry: Not yet, but maybe someday! I passed my monster exams!

Moe: Wow! Way to go! I know you were studying hard for those. You got kind of hung up on the science of hiding under the bed, and I wasn't sure if you would ever figure it out. You deserve a lot of praise! Way to go! Great job!

Harry: Thank you for the praise!

Moe: I know somebody else that really deserves some praise!

Harry: God has done so much for us! He made us and He saved us from our sins! He made the whole world just for us! God deserves all the praise!

Moe: That's why *Psalms 9:1* says, *I will praise you, O LORD, with all my heart; I will tell of all your wonders.*

Harry: I just love *Psalms 9:1*! God deserves to be praised for all the wonderful things He has done for us. *I will praise you, O LORD, with all my heart; I will tell of all your wonders. Psalms 9:1.*

Moe: God deserves to be praised with ALL our heart, and He wants us to tell others about all the wonderful things He has done!

Harry: *Psalms 9:1, I will praise you, O LORD, with all my heart; I will tell of ALL your wonders. Psalms 9:1.*

Moe: It would take more than a monster long lifetime to tell of ALL the wonderful things God has done!

Harry: But we can live our life for Him and start by telling others about His wonderful gift of salvation. PRAISE! PRAISE! PRAISE!

Moe: *Psalms 9:1, I will praise you, O LORD, with all my heart; I will tell of all your wonders.*

Harry: *Pslams 9:1, I will praise you, O LORD, with all my heart; I will tell of all your wonders.* I gotta go tell somebody about how wonderful God is! (exit)

Moe: I'm with ya on that! (exit)